Arise AND Conquer

YOU ARE THE COMMANDER OF YOUR DAY

devotional

MICHELLE CHAVIS

Acknowledgments

I thank GOD for being faithful even when I was not, and for the vision to impact the lives of others.

To my children, Laticia and Trevon for their unconditional love, encouragement and patience. Laticia, thank you for the gift of my Glam-Daughter "Princess Jadah", she is a complete bundle of JOY. My mom, children & Glam-daughter are literally the "Wind Beneath My Wings."

To my aunties Donna Bullock & Gloria Chavis & Pam Tabron, thanks for believing in me & your continued support.

To Jocelyn Campbell Thompson for being consistent in supporting me & believing in me.

To Shavonna Futrell, thank you for being my right hand, I know I can always count on you.

To Tonya Bullock, Cynthia Moore, Torrie Stanley, Asha Wade, Teresa Bobbitt, Toya Mayes, Keshia Sharpe, Emmy Preiss, Michelle Lawton & Karen Epps Watson thank you all for being a source of motivation.

To my "literary midwife," Jacquelin Thomas, thank you for helping me pursue my purpose.

To my literary jewels thank you for being a source of inspiration Kimberly Lawson Roby, (Auntie) Michelle Stimpson, Vanessa Miller Pierce,

Rhonda McKnight, Renee Daniel Flager, EN Joy, Lasheera Lee & Brian W Smith (my favorite male author).

To my Spiritual mothers, June Moore & Patricia Alston-Tapp, thank you for covering, encouraging me, and always pushing me.

To my classmate Debra Skinner - thanks for believing what GOD said about me & the rest of my Satellite East classmates - we were destined to become EAGLES.

To Victorious Ladies Reading Book Club, thank you for your continued support & allowing me to be your president.

To Rebecca Pau, thank for bringing my vision to reality.

Last but never least, to Venita Alderman, thank you for Bossing me, when I didn't want to be Bossed. LOL. You helped me all the way through this "literary pregnancy" & I can't thank you enough.

"'His Lord said to him,"Well done, good and faithful servant; you have been faithful over a few things, I will make you ruler over many things. Enter into the joy of your Lord.'"

Matthew 25:23 NKJV

dedicated to

YVONNE CHAVIS FORD
JANUARY 2, 1953 - JULY 16, 2013

No amount of monetary wealth could ever compare to the spiritual wealth I gained from you. Your nurturing has given me the strength to persevere and achieve my goals. Your unconditional love, support, positive affirmations, prayers, and even correction when it was needed are the reasons I have become the woman that I am.

Your legacy of Faith, Hope & Love still live on because of the seeds you planted. Trust in the LORD is what you would always say & that is what I will always do.

I love & miss you dearly.

ARISE & CONQUER

Your DESTINY is NOT connected to PEOPLE, it's connected to PURPOSE.

#Arise&Conquer
#PursueThat
#ThePurposePusher
#Elevation
#EaglesSoar

"In Him also we have obtained an inheritance, being predestined according to the purpose of Him who works all things according to the counsel of His will."

Ephesians 1:11

GOD empty me of ME & FILL me with you. GOD, I am grateful & humble to be used for your Glory. As I embark on this new journey, I pray for your continued Wisdom & Guidance, for I am nothing without YOU.

#ThePurposePusher
#WithHoldingNothing

The Spirit of the Lord is on me, because he has anointed me to proclaim good news to the poor. He has sent me to proclaim freedom for the prisoners and recovery of sight for the blind, to set the oppressed free.

Luke 4:18 NIV

Affirmations

I have a new mind set, new mercies, new thinking, new favor, renewed strength. I'm ready to CONQUER this day! #declaration

Your Affirmation:

____

____

____

____

____

____

____

____

____

____

____

____

I declare and decree that this is the year of restoration, and all that I have sown in tears, I shall reap in joy. #declaration

Your Affirmation:

____

____

____

____

____

____

____

____

____

____

____

____

I am a chosen vessel, I am destined to be successful, I am above and not beneath, I am the head and not the tail, by the power of the blood I've been redeemed, I am not conceited but I am content with Christ in my life I will always win, and no matter what, I will forever love the skin that I am in, because I am a chosen vessel and I'm destined to be successful. #declaration

Your Affirmation:

____

____

____

____

____

____

____

____

____

I am strong in the LORD and in His mighty power. His grace is making me wiser and stronger. #declaration

Your Affirmation:

____

____

____

____

____

____

____

____

____

____

____

____

Sickness cannot dwell in me; the number of my days GOD shall fulfill. GOD is watching over his WORD to perform it and Jehovah RAPHA is my healer. #declaration

Your Affirmation:

____

____

____

____

____

____

____

____

____

____

I declare and decree I will not be moved by what I see but by my FAITH in GOD and his WORD. I will see my situation through the eyes of GOD and every thought that exalts itself against the WORD of GOD will be paralyzed in the name of JESUS!!! #declaration

Your Affirmation:

____

____

____

____

____

____

____

____

____

____

____

The gift of God is stirred up in me therefore I shall live victoriously. #declaration

Your Affirmation:

____

____

____

____

____

____

____

____

____

____

____

I walk in authority and everywhere my feet shall tread upon shall be blessed. #declaration

Your Affirmation:

____

____

____

____

____

____

____

____

____

____

____

This is the day that The Lord has made, and I will have abundance, excess and overflow in every area of my life. #declaration

Your Affirmation:

____

____

____

____

____

____

____

____

____

____

____

____

Every wicked scheme and attack that attempted to come my way is paralyzed in the name of Jesus. #declaration

Your Affirmation:

____

____

____

____

____

____

____

____

____

____

____

____

____

The Holy Spirit hovers me and the angels are protecting me I SHALL NOT FEAR!!! #declaration

Your Affirmation:

____

____

____

____

____

____

____

____

____

____

I bind every thought that is contrary to the voice of GOD!! I am Kingdom minded.
#declaration

Your Affirmation:

I have peace in the midst of my storm,
because my mind is stayed on Jesus. #declaration

Your Affirmation:

I serve a God who is able to do anything but fail, so his plans for me will always succeed. #declaration

Your Affirmation:

____

____

____

____

____

____

____

____

____

____

If God be for me the WHO doesn't matter,
because GOD got me. #declaration

Your Affirmation:

____

____

____

____

____

____

____

____

____

____

It doesn't matter what you say about me
God has already spoken over me. #declaration

Your Affirmation:

____

____

____

____

____

____

____

____

____

____

____

I dwell in the secret place of the highest (GOD), therefore I am protected from all hurt, harm and danger. #declaration

Your Affirmation:

____

____

____

____

____

____

____

____

____

____

____

I will not worry but I will meditate on the word of God. #declaration

Your Affirmation:

____

____

____

____

____

____

____

____

____

____

____

This is the day that the LORD has made, and I will not have lack in any area of my life. My mind is renewed, and my heart is receptive to the things of GOD. #declaration

Your Affirmation:

____

____

____

____

____

____

____

____

____

____

I declare and decree that no weapon formed against me shall prosper Jehovah NISSI is fighting my battles for me. #declaration

Your Affirmation:

____

____

____

____

____

____

____

____

____

____

____

I declare and decree that any thought contrary to the will of GOD be consumed and I will think on those things that are pure, lovely and of a good report. #declaration

Your Affirmation:

____

____

____

____

____

____

____

____

____

____

____

Purpose
Points

Our words are powerful & they shape our atmosphere, two of the most powerful words we can say is "I AM", when you attach I AM, whatever you put behind it will try to attach to you, Jesus used the same saying "I AM" in seven declarations about Himself.

In all seven, He combines I AM to show his significance, to the world in the book of John.

They are I AM the Bread of Life, I AM the Light of the World, I AM the Door of the Sheep, I AM the Good Shepherd, I AM the Resurrection and the Life, I AM the Way, the Truth and the Life, I AM the True Vine.

WHO I AM
I AM A PURPOSE PUSHER
I AM A LEADER
I AM A SMILE GIVER
I AM POSITIVE
I AM SUCCESSFUL
I AM INFLUENTIAL
I AM CONFIDENT
I AM AN ENCOURAGER
I AM VICTORIOUS
I AM A DIFFERENCE MAKER

WHO ARE YOU

I AM:

I am the COMMANDER of My day therefore I will SPEAK into the Atmosphere what GOD says about ME. Knowing that my PRAISE is a mass weapon of destruction to every chain that wants to bind Me. I Praise GOD in The Midst Of & In Spite Of because the VICTORY IS MINE & In the End I WIN.

#LetGODBeGOD
#Arise&Conquer

"So, shall they fear the name of the LORD from the west, And His glory from the rising of the sun; When the enemy comes in like a flood, The Spirit of the LORD will lift up a standard against him."

Isaiah 59:19 NKJV

I am the commander of my day and I

command:_________________________________

Whenever you're trying to figure out "How am I going to get through this?" Just take a moment to read GOD's Resume.

#GODIsAble

"Now to Him who is able to do exceedingly abundantly above all that we ask or think, according to the power that works in us."
Ephesians 3:20 NKJV

I am the commander of my day and I command:_______________________________

____

____

____

____

____

____

____

____

____

____

____

____

I am the COMMANDER of My day therefore
I know there is nothing that I can CONFESS, to
make GOD love me less. My Breakthrough is NOT
in what I SEE but in what I SAY.

#John3:16

"For God so loved the world that He gave
His only begotten Son, that whoever believes in
Him should not perish but have everlasting life."
John 3:16 NKJV

I am the commander of my day and I

command:_______________________________

GOD Is Establishing order in my life & I am Embracing My New Season, "DUE SEASON". I shall move from WORDS to ACTIONS, I shall move from DREAMS to REALITY & I shall move from PROMISE to POSSESSION.

#LetGODBeGOD
#DUESeason
#Arise&Conquer

"The steps of a good man are ordered by the LORD, And He delights in his way. Though he falls, he shall not be utterly cast down; For the LORD upholds him with His hand."

Psalms 37:23-24 NKJV

I am the commander of my day and I

command:_______________________________________

If it was too late, you wouldn't be breathing. The dream GOD gave you is still ATTAINABLE. SAY what you SEEK, until you SEE what you SPEAK.

#NeverGiveUp
#DeliberateLiving
#Arise&Conquer

"So, Jesus answered and said to them, "Have faith in God. For assuredly, I say to you, whoever says to this mountain, 'Be removed and be cast into the sea,' and does not doubt in his heart, but believes that those things he says will be done, he will have whatever he says. Therefore, I say to you, whatever things you ask when you pray, believe that you receive them, and you will have them."

Mark 11:22-24 NKJV

I am the commander of my day and I

command:___________________________________

____

____

____

____

____

____

____

____

____

____

____

We often tend to want more for people than they want for themselves. I've learned that sometimes you must settle for a watered seed & let GOD do the growing.

#LetGo&LetGOD
#Arise&Conquer

"Keep your heart with all diligence, for out of it spring the issues of life."

Proverbs 4:23 NKJV

I am the commander of my day and I command:_______________________________________

____

____

____

____

____

____

____

____

____

____

____

____

You're not the only stick in GOD's matchbox, but you're the one GOD picked to strike and light the dark spaces.

#YouWerePredestined
#Arise&Conquer

"For we are His workmanship, created in Christ Jesus for good works, which God prepared beforehand that we should walk in them."
                                        Ephesians 2:10 NKJV

I am the commander of my day and I

command:_______________________________________

____

____

____

____

____

____

____

____

____

____

____

____

Be MINDFUL of WHAT & WHO You Allow to RENT Space in Your MIND. If "IT" Or THEY" Don't Serve A POSITIVE Purpose, It's Time To EVICT!!! You Are the LANDLORD of Your MIND.

#evaluateyourMENTALlease
#Arise&Conquer

"Finally, brethren, whatever things are true, whatever things are noble, whatever things are just, whatever things are pure, whatever things are lovely, whatever things are of good report, if there is any virtue and if there is anything praiseworthy—meditate on these things."

Philippians 4:8 NKJV

I am the commander of my day and I

command:________________________________

____

____

____

____

____

____

____

____

____

____

____

____

When the Enemy Is Pushing Your Buttons CHANGE The " ACCESS CODE ". Remember It's Just A COMMERCIAL Advertising the Depth of Your STRENGTH! CHANGE the CHANNEL and Stay Focused.

"The LORD will perfect that which concerns me; Your mercy, O LORD, endures forever; Do not forsake the works of Your hands."

Psalms 138:8 NKJV

I am the commander of my day and I

command:_______________________________

Whenever you are discouraged, disappointed or dismayed know that GOD can turn your ADVERSITY into VICTORY. The story of Joseph teaches us that even when we are in a VALLEY situation GOD can elevate us to a MOUNTAIN where we will be on top.

#Genesis37-42
#Great&MightyIsOurGOD
#SetBackToBeSetUp
#Favor
#ConstantlyBlessME
#LetGODBeGOD

I am the commander of my day and I

command:_______________________________________

____

____

____

____

____

____

____

____

____

____

____

____

Use your GOD given COMMON SENSE to remove NON-SENSE so that your life can make SENSE. Energy is contagious so protect your space. You are the commander of your day, therefore command your atmosphere.

"And do not be conformed to this world, but be transformed by the renewing of your mind, that you may prove what is that good and acceptable and perfect will of God."

Romans 12:2 NKJV

I am the commander of my day and I

command:________________________________

____

____

____

____

____

____

____

____

____

____

____

____

Satan and his demons are beneath me. I am too important to give my time to what's beneath me! Laughing in the face of the enemy.

#FocusForward
#PowerAndAuthority

"Behold, I give you the authority to trample on serpents and scorpions, and over all the power of the enemy, and nothing shall by any means hurt you."

Luke 10:19 NKJV

I am the commander of my day and I

command:_______________________________

____

____

____

____

____

____

____

____

____

____

____

____

I am too VALUABLE to entertain situations that insult my INTELLIGENCE. When I was a child, I spoke as a child, I understood as a child, I thought as a child: but when I became an ADULT, I put away childish things & people.

"And do not be conformed to this world, but be transformed by the renewing of your mind, that you may prove what is that good and acceptable and perfect will of God."

Romans 12:2 NKJV

I am the commander of my day and I

command:_______________________________

____

____

____

____

____

____

____

____

____

____

____

____

____

My content is greater than my context, therefore, GOD has given me the capacity to conquer the chaos.

"Being confident of this very thing, that He who has begun a good work in you will complete it until the day of Jesus Christ."

Philippians 1:6 NKJV

I am the commander of my day and I

command:__________________________________

____

____

____

____

____

____

____

____

____

____

____

____

GOD is faithful to perform his WORD. Any day now he is going to do just what he said.

#Patience

"The Lord is not slack concerning His promise, as some count slackness, but is longsuffering toward us, not willing that any should perish but that all should come to repentance."

II Peter 3:9 NKJV

I am the commander of my day and I

command:____

There is JOY in knowing that anything GOD connects to you, will eventually be drawn to you. You just must IGNORE the KNOCKOFFS!!!

"Having a form of godliness but denying its power. And from such people turn away!"
II Timothy 3:5 NKJV

I am the commander of my day and I

command:_______________________________________

____

____

____

____

____

____

____

____

____

____

____

____

The enemy thought he was going to burn me, but GOD used the fire to BLESS me. You can't kill what's ANOINTED to LIVE.

"When you pass through the waters, I will be with you; And through the rivers, they shall not overflow you. When you walk through the fire, you shall not be burned, Nor shall the flame scorch you. For I am the LORD your God, The Holy One of Israel, your Savior; I gave Egypt for your ransom, Ethiopia and Seba in your place."

Isaiah 43:2-3 NKJV

I am the commander of my day and I

command:_________________________________

____

____

____

____

____

____

____

____

____

____

____

____

Thank you, LORD, for another day. I know I am not PERFECT, but I am PLIABLE. Continue to work in & on me for your Glory.

"Create in me a clean heart, O God, and renew a steadfast spirit within me. Do not cast me away from Your presence, and do not take Your Holy Spirit from me. Restore to me the joy of Your salvation, And uphold me by Your Generous Spirit."

Psalms 51:10-12 NKJV

I am the commander of my day and I

command:_______________________________

____

____

____

____

____

____

____

____

____

____

____

____

NEVER get sidetracked by people that are NOT on track. People will wish you the BEST then hate when you have it.

"Do not be deceived: "Evil company corrupts good habits."

I Corinthians 15:33 NKJV

I am the commander of my day and I

command:_______________________________________

Even when the SUN don't shine, I KNOW that the SON still shines on ME.

#SONShine

"The LORD makes His face shine upon you, And be gracious to you; The LORD lifts up His countenance upon you, and give you peace."

Numbers 6:25-26 NKJV

I am the commander of my day and I command:____

____

____

____

____

____

____

____

____

____

____

____

____

I am the COMMANDER of my day, therefore I declare & decree that NOTHING or NO ONE will disturb my INNER PEACE.

#GREATERIsWithinInME

"You will keep him in perfect peace, whose mind is stayed on You, because he trusts in You."

Isaiah 26:3 NKJV

I am the commander of my day and I

command:_______________________________

PEACE, POWER & PROSPERITY flow easily out of the Presence of GOD when WE decide to get in the PRESENCE of GOD.

"You will show me the path of life; In Your presence is fullness of joy; At Your right hand are pleasures forevermore."

Psalms 16:11 NKJV

I am the commander of my day and I

command:_________________________________

I want to encourage you to never live your life according to other people time table. Your biggest accomplishment in life will be doing what others say you couldn't & wouldn't do. You might not get there today, tomorrow, in six months or even a year but know that when you KNOW your PURPOSE, PLAN for it & PURSUE it you will get there with GOD as your Guide. I BELIEVE IN YOU.

#ThePurposePusher
#PurposeDriven
#LiveOnPurpose

"And we know that all things work together for good to those who love God, to those who are the called according to His purpose."

Romans 8:28 NKJV

I am the commander of my day and I command:_______________________________

GOD was in the middle of everything, as I know today. Even in my mess, GOD was there because he kept me enough to be able to be standing here today in my sound mind, to be able to know that His hand is on my life. The most important thing that GOD has done in me, He saved me and I'm free. I'm a free woman, not only in the society, But I'm a free woman in GOD You don't have to be in Prison to be a Prisoner.

#IHearTheChainsFalling
#WomanThouArtLoosed
#Purpose

"I called on the LORD in distress; The LORD answered me and set me in a broad place. The LORD is on my side; I will not fear. What can man do to me?"

Psalms 118:5-6 NKJV

I am the commander of my day and I

command:____________________________________

GOD chose ME and there is nothing anyone can do to take that away from ME!

"I will praise You, for I am fearfully and wonderfully made; Marvelous are Your works, and that my soul knows very well."

Psalms 139:14 NKJV

I am the commander of my day and I

command:_________________________________

____

____

____

____

____

____

____

____

____

____

____

____

If the people in your life can't handle your TRANSFORMATION, they aren't ready to GO with you to your DESTINATION.

"He who walks with wise men will be wise, But the companion of fools will be destroyed."
Proverbs 13:20 NKJV

I am the commander of my day and I

command:______________________________

____

____

____

____

____

____

____

____

____

____

____

____

YOU are the Commander of your day, so Speak into the Atmosphere & Command it. Remember with GOD, you can do what others thought you couldn't do!!!

#TakeTheLimitsOff
#Purpose
#Speak
#Declare&Decree

"Be anxious for nothing, but in everything by prayer and supplication, with thanksgiving, let your requests be made known to God; and the peace of God, which surpasses all understanding, will guard your hearts and minds through Christ Jesus."

Philippians 4:6-7 NKJV

I am the commander of my day and I command:_______________________________

GOD thank you for reminding me that as long as I have a PULSE, I have a PURPOSE & you have a PLAN.

#ThePurposePusher

"Trust in the LORD with all your heart, And lean not on your own understanding; In all your ways acknowledge Him, And He shall direct your paths."

Proverbs 3:5-6 NKJV

I am the commander of my day and I

command:__________________________________

Never limit your goals because someone is uncomfortable with your success. GOD has predestined you for Greatness, go forth & embrace the Champion within you.

"Delight yourself also in the LORD, And He shall give you the desires of your heart. Commit your way to the LORD, Trust also in Him, And He shall bring it to pass."

Psalms 37:4-5 NKJV

I am the commander of my day and I

command:_______________________________________

____

____

____

____

____

____

____

____

____

____

____

____

Your MOOD belongs to you, DON'T give it to the devil. Let emotions subside & then decide.

#CommandYourDay
#TransformYourMind
#ThinkBeforeYouSpeak

"A fool vents all his feelings, but a wise man holds them back."

Proverbs 29:11 NKJV

I am the commander of my day and I command:_______________________________

____

____

____

____

____

____

____

____

____

____

____

____

____

GOD is PERFECTING those things that concern ME. Those that have plotted or prayed for my ELIMINATION, will have to bear witness of my ELEVATION.

#DueSeason

"When a man's ways please the LORD, He makes even his enemies to be at peace with him."
Proverbs 16:7 NKJV

I am the commander of my day and I

command:______________________________

____

____

____

____

____

____

____

____

____

____

____

____

Surround yourself with those that STRENGTHEN your WEAKNESS, NOT those that WEAKEN your STRENGTH!

"Blessed is the man Who walks not in the counsel of the ungodly, nor stands in the path of sinners, nor sits in the seat of the scornful; But his delight is in the law of the LORD, And in His law, he meditates day and night. He shall be like a tree Planted by the rivers of water, that brings forth its fruit in its season, whose leaf also shall not wither; And whatever he does shall prosper."

Psalms 1:1-3 NKJV

I am the commander of my day and I

command:_______________________________

____

____

____

____

____

____

____

____

____

____

____

____

____

There are those that PRAY for you and others that PREY on you. Pray for discernment.

"He who walks with integrity walks securely, but he who perverts his ways will become known."

Proverbs 10:9 NKJV

I am the commander of my day and I

command:_________________________________

____

____

____

____

____

____

____

____

____

____

____

____

Your concept of your reality, is shaped by your thoughts. Therefore, train your mind to hear what GOD is whispering, instead of what the enemy is shouting.

"Commit your works to the LORD, and your thoughts will be established."

Proverbs 16:3 NKJV

I am the commander of my day and I command:____

____

____

____

____

____

____

____

____

____

____

____

Trials & Tribulations will come but even when I am in the HEAT, I know who controls the thermostat.

#MiracleWorker

"And when he came to the den, he cried out with a lamenting voice to Daniel. The king spoke, saying to Daniel, "Daniel, servant of the living God, has your God, whom you serve continually, been able to deliver you from the lions?" Then Daniel said to the king, "O king, live forever! My God sent His angel and shut the lions' mouths, so that they have not hurt me, because I was found innocent before Him; and also, O king, I have done no wrong before you." Now the king was exceedingly glad for him, and commanded that they should take Daniel up out of the den. So, Daniel was taken up out of the den, and no injury whatever was found on him, because he believed in his God."

Daniel 6:20-23 NKJV

I am the commander of my day and I command:____________________________________

I Pray that in this season you will stop
COUNTING what's in your hand, and start
TRUSTING who's hands you're in.

#Isaiah49:16
#JehovahJireh

"See, I have inscribed you on the palms of
My hands; Your walls are continually before Me."
Isaiah 49:16 NKJV

I am the commander of my day and I

command:______________________________

____

____

____

____

____

____

____

____

____

____

____

____

Favorite Scriptures

"For I know the plans I have for you," declares the LORD, "plans to prosper you and not to harm you, plans to give you hope and a future."

Jeremiah 29:11

"But they that wait upon the Lord shall renew their strength; they shall mount up with wings as eagles; they shall run, and not be weary; and they shall walk, and not faint."

Isaiah 40: 31

"From the west, people will fear the name of the LORD, and from the rising of the sun, they will revere his glory. For he will come like a pent-up flood that the breath of the LORD drives along."

Isaiah 59:19

"Take delight in the LORD, and he will give you the desires of your heart."

Psalm 37:4

"The LORD will vindicate me; your love, LORD,
endures forever- do not abandon the works of
your hands."

Psalm 138:8

"The LORD is my shepherd, I lack nothing.
2   He makes me lie down in green pastures,
he leads me beside quiet waters,
3   he refreshes my soul.
He guides me along the right paths
   for his name's sake.
4 Even though I walk
   through the darkest valley,
I will fear no evil,
   for you are with me;
your rod and your staff,
   they comfort me.

5 You prepare a table before me
   in the presence of my enemies.
You anoint my head with oil;
   my cup overflows.
6 Surely your goodness and love will follow me
   all the days of my life,
and I will dwell in the house of the LORD
   forever."

Psalm 23

"Whoever dwells in the shelter of the Most High
    will rest in the shadow of the Almighty.
[2] I will say of the LORD, "He is my refuge and my fortress,
    my God, in whom I trust."

[3] Surely he will save you
    from the fowler's snare
    and from the deadly pestilence.
[4] He will cover you with his feathers,
    and under his wings you will find refuge;
    his faithfulness will be your shield and rampart.
[5] You will not fear the terror of night,
    nor the arrow that flies by day,
[6] nor the pestilence that stalks in the darkness,
    nor the plague that destroys at midday.
[7] A thousand may fall at your side,
    ten thousand at your right hand,
    but it will not come near you.
[8] You will only observe with your eyes
    and see the punishment of the wicked.

[9] If you say, "The LORD is my refuge,"
    and you make the Most High your dwelling,
[10] no harm will overtake you,
    no disaster will come near your tent.
[11] For he will command his angels concerning you
    to guard you in all your ways;
[12] they will lift you up in their hands,

    so that you will not strike your foot against a
stone.
13 You will tread on the lion and the cobra;
    you will trample the great lion and the serpent.

14 "Because he loves me," says the LORD, "I will
rescue him;
    I will protect him, for he acknowledges my
name.
15 He will call on me, and I will answer him;
    I will be with him in trouble,
    I will deliver him and honor him.
16 With long life I will satisfy him
    and show him my salvation."

Psalm 91

1 I lift up my eyes to the mountains—
    where does my help come from?
2 My help comes from the LORD,
    the Maker of heaven and earth.

3 He will not let your foot slip—
    he who watches over you will not slumber;
4 indeed, he who watches over Israel
    will neither slumber nor sleep.

5 The LORD watches over you—
    the LORD is your shade at your right hand;

^{6} the sun will not harm you by day,
   nor the moon by night.

^{7} The LORD will keep you from all harm—
   he will watch over your life;
^{8} the LORD will watch over your coming and going
   both now and forevermore."
Psalm 121

"And we know that in all things God works for the good of those who love him, who have been called according to his purpose." Romans 8:28

"Now to him who is able to do immeasurably more than all we ask or imagine, according to his power that is at work within us."
Ephesians 3:20

Your Favorite Scriptures:

____

____

____

____

____

Your Favorite Scriptures:

Your Favorite Scriptures:

____

____

____

____

____

____

____

Your Favorite Scriptures:

____

____

____

____

____

Your Favorite Scriptures:

Your Favorite Scriptures:

____

____

____

____

____

____

____

Your Favorite Scriptures:

____

____

____

____

____

____

____

____

____

Your Favorite Scriptures:

____

____

____

____

____

____

____

Your Favorite Scriptures:

____

Your Favorite Scriptures:

Your Favorite Scriptures:

~Arise & Conquer